Wheat Belly Slow Cooker Cookbook:

Top 90+ Delicious, and Easy-To-Cook for Busy Mom and Dad Wheat Belly Slow cooker Recipes for a Healthy Eating in the Real World.

By

Lisa Young

Copyright © 2019, By: *Lisa Young*

ISBN-13: 978-1-950772-90-2
ISBN-10: 1-950772-90-X

All Rights Reserved. No part of this publication may be reproduced in any form or by any means, including scanning, photocopying, or otherwise without prior written permission of the copyright holder.

Disclaimer:

The information provided in this book is designed to provide helpful information on the subjects discussed. The publisher and author are not responsible for any specific health or allergy needs that may require medical supervision and are not liable for any damages or negative consequences from any treatment, action, application or preparation, to any person reading or following the information in this book.

Table of Contents

Introduction to the wheat belly slow cooker Cookbook 6

Recipes to help you lose the wheat, lose the weight and find your path back to a healthy you 8

    Crock Pot Chicken and Chickpea Curry 8

    Crock Pot Chicken Parmesan 9

    Pot roast 10

    Crockpot Chicken Spaghetti Sauce 12

    Arroz con glandules 13

    Wheat Belly Flaxseed Wrap 15

    Easy Mexican Chicken Crock-Pot Chowder 17

    Crock Pot Roast Chicken 18

    Chili 19

    Youngn Hearty Lentils & Wild Rice 20

    Chicken Cacciatore Slow Cooker 21

    Crock Pot Sweet 'n Sour Chicken over Rice 22

    Green Chili Stew 24

    Crock Pot Soup: Chicken, Vegetable & Rice Soup 25

    Pulled Pork 26

    Crock Pot Sweet Potato and Apples 27

    Cleansing Veggie Soup 29

    Crock Pot Soup: Chicken, Vegetable and Rice Soup 31

    Diet Coke Chicken 32

    Beef Tips in Crockpot 33

    Turkey breast meatloaf 34

    Pork Chops with Jalapeno-Pecan Cornbread Stuffing 35

    Turkey Stew 37

    Homemade Refried Beans 38

    Cashew chicken 39

    Chicken Enchilada Chili 41

Crock Pot Stew with Brown Rice	42
Roxie's Calico Beans	43
Apple Cinnamon Crock Pot Oatmeal	45
Slow Cooker Chicken Tacos	47
Crockpot Crazy Chicken	48
Slow Cooker Pork Loin with Creamy Sauce	49
Low Sodium Mexican Chicken Stew in Slow Cooker	50
Turkey & Veggie Meal	52
Chicken with Cheesy Mushroom Gravy	54
Low fat Cheeseburger Pie	56
Slow-Cooker Salsa Chicken	58
Crock Pot Sour Cream and Onion Chicken	59
Thai Chicken with Peanut Sauce	61
Cowboy Chicken	62
Stacey's Crock-pot Chicken and Dumplings	63
Crock-pot Chicken Ragu (slow cooker)	64
Slow Cooker Barbecue Orange Chicken	66
Crock Pot Chicken Cacciatore (Low Sodium)	67
Slow Cooker Garlic Tomato Chicken	69
Pork and Potatoes in Mustard Sauce	71
Easy Slow Cooker Lemony Garlic Chicken Breast	73
Slow-Cooker Chicken Paprikash	75
Crock pot macaroni and cheese	77
Slow Cooked Chicken Breast with Peppers	78
Maple Flavored Barbeque Chicken - Crock Pot	79
Pork Chops for the Slow Cooker	80
Slow cooker beef barley vegetable soup	81
Slow Cooker Honey Mustard Chicken	83
Slow Cooker Bourbon Street Chicken	85

Black Bean Chicken 87

Slow Cooker Pork Chop Dinner 88

Slow Cooker Rotisserie Chicken 90

Slow Cooker Kentucky Burgoo 93

Slow Cooker Beef Roast with Vegetables 95

Slow Cooker Marinara Chicken and Vegetables 97

Slow Cooker Creamy Paprika Pork 99

BONUS RECIPE 101

Crock Pot Salmon Fillets and Vegetables 101

Crock Pot Buffalo Chicken Lettuce Wraps 102

Slow Cooker Jalapeño Popper Chicken Chili 104

Crock Pot Sesame Honey Chicken 106

Slow Cooker Lemon Feta Drumsticks 108

Embarrassingly Easy Crock Pot Salsa Chicken Thighs 109

Crock Pot Balsamic Pork Roast 110

Crock Pot Santa Fe Chicken 111

Easy Crock Pot Chicken and Black Bean Taco Salad 112

Slow Cooker Taco Stew Meat 114

Fish Tacos with Mango Salsa 115

Easy Shredded Pork over Caramelized Plantains 116

Crock Pot Kid-Friendly Turkey Chili 118

Honey Chili Chicken and Vegetables 120

Easy Creamy Crock-Pot Chicken Tikka Masala 122

Lighter Buffalo Chicken Dip 124

CONCLUSION 125

Introduction to the wheat belly slow cooker Cookbook

Lose the Wheat, Lose the Weight, and Find Your Path Back to Health!

As a strong advocate of the *"**GRAIN BRAIN" by Dr. David Perl mutter's and "WHEAT BELLY"*** by Dr. William Davis' runaway New York Times bestselling book. My sole aim for this book is to empower you with powerful dieting plan that cut through the misinterpretations, misconceptions, misleading marketing, and bad science that passes as nutritional and health information.

Dr. William Davis a renowned cardiologist explains how eliminating wheat from our day to day diets can prevent fat storage, shrink unsightly bulges, and reverse myriad health problems. Therefore, the sole purpose of this book is to help you make that change today and break weight plateau, reverse autoimmune conditions such as rheumatoid arthritis and Cohn's disease, fully reverse diabetes and other metabolic disorders and create a grain-free lifestyle without having to sacrifice your nutrition, variety, or taste.

Wheat Belly is specifically about two things which is eliminating wheat (and other gluten-containing grains such as barley and rye), and on the other hand managing carbohydrates/sugars to individual tolerance levels to manage blood sugar and promote weight-loss if desired. Wheat Belly is not all about being "gluten-free" for there is much wrong with wheat of which gluten is only a part. I will strongly recommend that people avoid gluten-free foods made with other high-carbohydrate grains, because that is inconsistent with achieving point #2!

Over 80% of the people are pre-diabetic or diabetic. So in an effort to reduce blood sugar which is of the increase, I asked patients to remove all wheat products from their diet based on the simple fact that, with few exceptions, foods made of wheat flour raise blood sugar higher than nearly all other foods. That is true for even whole grains.

However, wheat Belly has become a phenomenon that countless thousands of people are following. It is more of a lifestyle choice or *manner* of eating. It is a passive diet that focus on eliminating certain foods as opposed to doing specific things. It is not based on calorie restriction and exercise. Nevertheless, there are alternative ways of preparing the foods we have come to love, without the guilt!

If you live a wheat free live I assure you for the first time in your live you will see the stark causality between what you eat and the status of your health. However, it can be quite an epiphany for people to eliminate a seemingly innocuous food and in a matter of a few days experience great health benefits or a rapid weight loss. As a matter of fact this initial experience *changes* people, and changes their attitude about and perception of food.

This *wheat belly slow cooker* is meant to be your day by day, meal by meal guide that guides you on how to eliminate grains from your life. This book will work you through the entire process of adopting a grain-free lifestyle, from purging your kitchens of grains, to shopping for wholesome foods, to making grain-free recipes. It offer a variety of recipes for all types of meals, ranging from breakfasts, mains dishes, side dishes, desserts, snacks, and some special occasion menus. You will learn many things that will allow you to live better and healthier and reduce your weight for live.

Recipes to help you lose the wheat, lose the weight and find your path back to a healthy you

Crock Pot Chicken and Chickpea Curry

Prep time: 10 mins
Cook time: 8 hours
Total time: 8 hours 10 mins
Serves: 4-6

Ingredients

- 2-3 potatoes (cubed)
- 4 cloves garlic (minced)
- 2 tablespoons of red curry paste
- 1 teaspoon of red pepper flakes
- ½ teaspoon of freshly ground black pepper
- 1 (12.5 ounce) can chickpeas (rinsed and drained)
- 2 chicken breasts (cubed)
- 1 onion (thinly sliced)
- 1 (24-ounce) can tomatoes (whole, diced, crushed, whatever you prefer - I used whole and crushed them with the back of a wooden spoon)
- 1 tablespoon of curry powder
- 1 teaspoon of kosher salt
- 1 1-inch piece fresh ginger (grated)
- 4 leaves fresh basil, thinly sliced (or better still chiffonier, for you fancy folks)

Directions:

1. First, you throw all of your ingredients into the crock pot, then stir to combine.
2. After which you set it on high for 4 hours, or on low for 8 hours.
3. At this point, when it's done, add in the rinsed chickpeas, stir to combine, and let it sit for 5 minutes to heat through.
4. Then you serve alone, or with rice or pita.
5. Enjoy!

Crock Pot Chicken Parmesan

Number of Servings: 6

Ingredients

28 oz. of can crushed tomatoes
1 (4oz) of can sliced black olives (it is optional)
2 teaspoons of oregano
6 oz. of mozzarella cheese
1 ½ lbs. of boneless, skinless chicken breast
2 cloves of garlic (minced)
4 oz. of sliced mushrooms (it is optional)
2 teaspoons of basil
1 teaspoon of thyme

Directions

1. First, you cut the chicken breasts into 4 oz. serving size and place in crock.
2. After which in a bowl, you mix the tomatoes, olives, mushrooms, garlic and spices.
3. After that, you pour over chicken and spread evenly.
4. Then you push down while spreading to ensure the sauce flows around the chicken.
5. At this point, you set crock pot to low and cook for about 8 - 10 hours.
6. Five minutes before serving, I suggest you place 1 ounce of mozzarella on each piece of chicken and allow to melt.
7. Finally, you serve with whole wheat pasta, if desired (preferably, you add about 200 calories for the pasta)

NUTRITIONAL INFORMATION

Serving Size: 6

Calories: 285.2

Total Fat: 8.0 g

Sodium: 565.0 mg

Total Carbs: 12.8 g

Dietary Fiber: 3.6 g

Protein: 41.0 g

Pot roast

Minutes to Prepare: *45*

Minutes to Cook: *330*

Number of Servings: *14*

Ingredients

4 small onion (cubed)
6 potatoes (cubed)
1 teaspoon of thyme
1 teaspoon of marjoram
2.4l of Beef Eye round roast (cubed)
1 lb. of carrots (sliced)
¼ cup of seasoned flour
1 teaspoon of basil
1 teaspoon of parsley

Directions

1. First, you put some water in the bottom of your crockpot.
2. After which you cube meat and season with seasoned flour.
3. After that, you process the other ingredients and add them to the crockpot.
4. This is when you stir or mix the ingredients.
5. Then you add more water until you can see it about 1 inch from the top.
6. Finally, you set crock on high and cook for 5-6 hours on high, longer on low.

NUTRITIONAL INFORMATION

Serving Size: 14

Calories: 344.6

Total Fat: 7.8 g

Sodium: 61.3 mg

Total Carbs: 40.8 g

Dietary Fiber: 5.7 g

Protein: 27.5 g

Crockpot Chicken Spaghetti Sauce

Minutes to Prepare: *5*

Minutes to Cook: *240*

Number of Servings: *16*

Ingredients
One jar tomato basil spaghetti sauce
1 Tablespoon of dried basil
3 cloves garlic
2 boneless skinless chicken breast (halves)
2 (about 15-oz) cans diced tomatoes
1 teaspoon of dried oregano

Directions

1. First, you place all the ingredients into a crockpot.
2. After which you cook on LOW for 6-8 hours.
3. After that, you remove chicken from crockpot and shred.
4. Then you return chicken to pot.
5. Remember that it makes 16 ½ -cup servings.
6. Finally, you serve over whole wheat pasta.

NUTRITIONAL INFORMATION

Serving Size: 16

Calories: 60.9

Total Fat: 1.2 g

Sodium: 211.4 mg

Total Carbs: 7.2 g

Dietary Fiber: 2.2 g

Protein: 5.2 g

Arroz con glandules

Tips:

Remember that you will need a big metal pot with cover

Number of Servings: 8

Ingredients
3 tablespoons of so Frito
½ cup of tomato sauce
6 Spanish olives (pitted)
One package sazon con cilantro yacoite (Goya)
1 can of Goya green pigeon peas
4 cups of Goya medium grain rice
3 Tablespoons of canola oil
2 tablespoons of cilantro (chopped finely)
1 oz. of pork belly, cut into tiny pieces (it is optional).
1 tablespoon of adobo (Goya)
1 tablespoon of onion powder
5 cups of water

Directions

1. First, you heat large pot over low heat.
2. After which you add oil, and pork belly.
3. After that, you add so Frito, tomato sauce, cilantro, olives, sazon, adobo, onion powder, pigeon peas (undrained).
4. Then you let simmer for about 3 minutes.
5. At this point, you add in rice and water bring heat up to medium- high mix and cover.
6. Furthermore, you let cook until water evaporates.
7. Finally, you put heat on low mix well and cover let simmer for additional 30 minutes or until rice is tender.
8. Serve warm.

NUTRITIONAL INFORMATION

Serving Size: 8

Calories: 222.9

Total Fat: 8.9 g

Sodium: 364.9 mg

Total Carbs: 30.9 g

Dietary Fiber: 0.6 g

Wheat Belly Flaxseed Wrap

Number of Servings: *1*

Tips

1. Remember that you can make this savory by adding herbs such as paprika, onion powder, garlic powder; or even non-caloric sweetener and cinnamon.
2. In the other hand, you can make this in a rectangular microwave safe dish, or a round container (I have used this sweetened lightly with sweetener and cinnamon as a pancake).
3. Make sure you serve with SF pancake syrup.

Ingredients

¼ teaspoon of baking powder
1 Tablespoon of water
3 Tablespoons of ground flaxseed
1 Tablespoon of coconut oil
1 large egg

Directions:

1. First, you mix together flax and baking powder.
2. After which you stir in melted coconut oil.
3. After that, you beat in egg and water until blended.
4. Then you pour into greased microwave safe pie plate.
5. At this point, you microwave on high for about 2-3 minutes until cooked.
6. After that, you allow to cool for about 5 minutes.
7. This is when you gently lift an edge with a spatula, loosen from the pan.
8. Finally, you flip the wrap over and top with desired toppings.

NUTRITIONAL INFORMATION

Serving Size: 1 wrap

Calories: 224.8

Total Fat: 20.4 g

Sodium: 176.9 mg

Total Carbs: 6.3 g

Dietary Fiber: 6.0 g

Protein: 8.5 g

Easy Mexican Chicken Crock-Pot Chowder

Number of Servings: 9

Ingredients

1 can of yellow corn
1 can (about 4oz) Fritos Jalapeno and Cheddar Cheese dip
1 cup of light sour cream
One can Cream of Chicken soup
1lb of boneless, skinless chicken breast
1 can of fat-free chicken broth
½ cup of canned green chilies

Directions:

1. First, you combine corn, cream of chicken, chicken broth, green chilies w/juice into crock-pot on low heat.
2. After which you add a pack of chopped chicken to crock-pot and cook for about 3-4hrs.
3. Then after 3-4hrs, in a separate bowl, mix 1 cup of the crock-pot mix with the sour cream and cheese dip and mix well.
4. Finally, you add the mixture to the crock-pot and cook for an additional 10-15mins.

NUTRITIONAL INFORMATION

Serving Size: 9

Calories: 116.8

Total Fat: 7.7 g

Sodium: 810.7 mg

Total Carbs: 10.3 g

Dietary Fiber: 0.6 g

Protein: 3.3 g

Crock Pot Roast Chicken

Number of Servings: 6

Ingredients

1 cup of water or better still low sodium-low fat chicken stock
1 clove of garlic minced
½ - 1 teaspoon of sweet paprika (enough for breast of chicken)
1 whole chicken 3-5lbs (better still see what will fit in your pot)
2 teaspoons of herb de province
1 small onion (sliced)

Directions:

1. First, you place the sliced onion in bottom of crock pot.
2. After which you skin chicken the best you can, removing any fat you can see, then place on top of onions.
3. After that, you pour water/stock over chicken.
4. Then you sprinkle garlic, herbs and paprika over top of chicken.
5. At this point, you cook on low for about 4-8 hours, chicken is done when leg pulls away smoothly.
6. Remember that this chicken will be pale so some men don't like the color that is why I use the Paprika to give it a little color.

    NOTE: older crock pots will take 6-8 hours newer ones can take 4-6 hours to cook)

NUTRITIONAL INFORMATION

Serving Size: 6

Calories: 77.1

Total Fat: 2.1 g

Sodium: 78.5 mg

Total Carbs: 2.0 g

Dietary Fiber: 0.2 g

Chili

Number of Servings: 6

Ingredients

1 cup of green pepper (chopped)
1 lb. of ground beef (lean)
1 cup onion (chopped)
4 cups of stewed tomatoes
1 tablespoon of chili powder
4 cups of kidney beans
1 tablespoon of cayenne
2 teaspoons of garlic

Directions

1. First, you brown the ground beef.
2. After which you put in crockpot.
3. After that, you sauté the onion, garlic and green pepper.
4. Then you add to crockpot.
5. In addition, you add kidney beans and stewed tomatoes.
6. After that, you stir in seasonings.
7. Finally, you cook on low in crockpot for 6 hours.

NOTE: you could add everything uncooked, but I'm Leary of that with ground beef.

I like the flavor of the sautéed onions, garlic and green bell pepper.

NUTRITIONAL INFORMATION

Serving Size: 6

Calories: 292.3

Total Fat: 9.0 g

Sodium: 811.5 mg

Total Carbs: 37.4 g

Dietary Fiber: 13.3 g

Protein: 17.3 g

Youngn Hearty Lentils & Wild Rice

Minutes to Prepare: *10*

Minutes to Cook: *180*

Number of Servings: *12*

Ingredients
1 cup of long grain wild rice
¼ cup of olive oil
1 small onion (chopped)
seas salt and fresh cracked pepper to taste
 1 ½ cups of dry lentils
5 cups of chicken broth
3 cloves garlic (pressed)
½ to 1 whole can Del Monte Diced Tomato w/ Onion & Garlic (it is optional)
1 teaspoon of Old Bay seasoning

Directions:

1. First, you throw all ingredients except seasonings into crock pot.
2. After which you turn on high for 1 ½ hours or low for 3 hours.
3. Then you add seasonings at the end, to preserve flavor.

NUTRITIONAL INFORMATION

Serving Size: 12

Calories: 99.9

Total Fat: 4.7 g

Sodium: 785.9 mg

Total Carbs: 11.5 g

Dietary Fiber: 2.8 g

Protein: 3.9 g

Chicken Cacciatore Slow Cooker

Minutes to Prepare: *15*

Minutes to Cook: *480*

Number of Servings: *12*

Ingredients
4 medium zucchini (cut up into 1 inch pieces)
12 oz. box of rotini pasta
2 lb. of chicken breasts
1 medium onion (cut up into wedges)
1 jar (about 26 oz.) spaghetti sauce

Directions

1. First, you place the chicken breasts, zucchini and onion into a slow cooker.
2. After which you pour in the sauce.
3. After that, you cook for 8 hours on low, or 4 hours on high.
4. Then you prepare the pasta as per the box directions.
5. Finally, you serve one cup of chicken mixture over 1 half cup of pasta.

NUTRITIONAL INFORMATION

Serving Size: 12

Calories: 222.7

Total Fat: 2.2 g

Sodium: 357.0 mg

Total Carbs: 27.5 g

Dietary Fiber: 3.7 g

Protein: 23.7 g

Crock Pot Sweet 'n Sour Chicken over Rice

Minutes to Prepare: *10*

Minutes to Cook: *470*

Number of Servings: *6*

Ingredients

1 medium onion (cut into wedges)
20-oz. of canned pineapple chunks
1 Tablespoon of low-sodium soy sauce
½ teaspoon of salt
¼ teaspoon of garlic powder
3 cups of cooked long grain rice (I used brown rice)
1 lb. baby carrots (or better still 4 carrots cleaned and sliced into chunks)
6 boneless, skinless chicken breast halves
1/3 cup packed brown sugar
2 teaspoons of chicken bouillon granules
½ teaspoon of ground ginger
3 tablespoons of cornstarch
¼ cup of water

Directions

1. First, you layer the carrots and onion in the bottom of the crock pot.
2. After which you top with chicken.
3. After that, you drain pineapple, reserving the juice.
4. Then you place on top of chicken; mix together the juice, brown sugar, soy sauce, chicken bouillon, salt, ginger, and garlic.
5. At this point, you pour over the top.
6. Furthermore, you cook on low 6-7 hours.
7. After that, you combine cornstarch and water then gradually stir into slow cooker.
8. This is when you cook for 30 minutes longer or until sauce is thickened.
9. Finally, you serve over cooked rice.

NOTE: makes 6 servings of ½ cup rice and 1 piece of chicken with ½ cup sauce.

NUTRITIONAL INFORMATION

Serving Size: 6

Calories: 341.1

Total Fat: 2.1 g

Sodium: 565.6 mg

Total Carbs: 56.5 g

Dietary Fiber: 3.7 g

Protein: 22.9 g

Green Chili Stew

Minutes to Prepare: *10*

Minutes to Cook: *360*

Number of Servings: *8*

Ingredients
1 can of Ro-Tel Diced Tomatoes and Chile Peppers
6 Medium Potatoes diced 2 inch squares (with or without skin)
Salt to taste (approx. 1 teaspoons)
Water
1 lb. fresh pork roast (Cubed)
½ cup of Roasted green Chile (can be mild, medium or hot).
½ Teaspoon of Garlic (NOTE: you may reduce Garlic to up to 1/3 teaspoon)
1/3 cup of Onions (it is optional)
Onion salt or powder can also be substituted.

Directions:

1. First, you combine all ingredient in a crock pot.
2. After which you fill Crock Pot to an inch from the top with water.
3. Then you cook for 6 hours.

NUTRITIONAL INFORMATION

Serving Size: 8

Calories: 208.8

Total Fat: 3.7 g

Sodium: 441.8 mg

Total Carbs: 27.3 g

Dietary Fiber: 2.1 g

Protein: 15.2 g

Crock Pot Soup: Chicken, Vegetable & Rice Soup

Minutes to Prepare: *20*

Minutes to Cook: *240*

Number of Servings: 6

Ingredients
2 Cups of Frozen Mixed Vegetables
4 Cups of College Inn Chicken Broth
1 Cup of Brown rice (makes about 3 ½ Cups cooked)
12oz of Chicken (cut into bite size pieces)

Directions

1. First, you put all the ingredients in the crock pot and leave it alone.

NOTE: I put the rice and chicken in the crock pot uncooked, it will cook during the day.

2. However, cooking times vary depending on your crock pot (mine cooked in 4 hours on high).
3. Remember that this recipe make 6 1C servings.
4. Enjoy!

NUTRITIONAL INFORMATION

Serving Size: 6

Calories: 207.0

Total Fat: 1.9 g

Sodium: 757.3 mg

Total Carbs: 31.3 g

Dietary Fiber: 2.7 g

Protein: 16.1 g

Pulled Pork

Number of Servings: 9

Ingredients

2 ¼ teaspoons of chili powder
1 ½ cups of barbecue sauce
1 ½ cups of onions (chopped)
2 ¼ lbs. of lean pork tenderloin

Directions

1. First, you combine onions, chili powder, barbecue sauce and pork in crock pot.
2. After which you cook on low for 6-8 hours or high for 3-4 hours.
3. After that, you shred with two forks (NOTE: Each serving is a ½ cup).

Optional: Serve in whole wheat hamburger bun (NOTE that it is not included in calorie count).

NUTRITIONAL INFORMATION

Serving Size: 9

Calories: 188.8

Total Fat: 3.2 g

Sodium: 7.4 mg

Total Carbs: 14.7 g

Dietary Fiber: 0.7 g

Protein: 24.4 g

Crock Pot Sweet Potato and Apples

Introduction

Tip:

1. However, sweet potatoes slow cooked with apples and spices in the crock pot makes for a healthy vegetarian and vegan side dish perfect for Thanksgiving or any day.
2. Remember, if your oven is full, make your sweet potatoes in the crockpot instead

Minutes to Prepare: *15*

Minutes to Cook: *300*

Number of Servings: *9*

Ingredients

3 apples (chopped)
2 tablespoons of brown sugar
¼ teaspoon of cinnamon
salt and pepper (to taste)
3 sweet potatoes (sliced or chopped)
¼ cup of maple syrup
2 tablespoons of margarine (melted)
¼ teaspoon of nutmeg

Directions

1. First. You cube sweet potatoes and apples.
2. After which you place them in a crock pot or slow cooker.
3. After that, you sprinkle remaining ingredients on top of the potatoes and apples.
4. Then you cook on low for 4 to 5 hours.
5. At this point, you add salt and pepper to taste.

NOTE: These easy sweet potatoes are wheat-free and gluten-free.

NUTRITIONAL INFORMATION

Serving Size: 9

Calories: 120.7

Total Fat: 2.9 g

Sodium: 15.1 mg

Total Carbs: 24.7 g

Dietary Fiber: 2.3 g

Protein: 0.8 g

Cleansing Veggie Soup

Number of Servings: *10*

Ingredients

Green onions (**NOTE:** I used quite a bit but the recipe called for three)
1 package of Lipton Chicken noodle soup mix
2 cans of green beans
2 green peppers
1 or 2 cans of stewed tomatoes
1 large can of beef broth
1 bunch of celery
2 lbs. of baby carrots

Directions

1. As for me I used a crock pot but it can be cooked on the stove as well.
2. First, you put all the non-fresh vegetables in the crock pot and turned it on high.
3. After which you cut the baby carrots in half and put them in a large pot on the stove in enough water to cover them.
4. Then you boil until soft.
5. At this point, while the carrots are boiling, I suggest you cut up the rest of the vegetables and set aside.
6. Then when the carrots are finished, you add them to the crock pot.
7. After that, you boil the rest of the vegetables in the carrot water.
8. Finally, when soft, add them to the crockpot as well as some or all of the water (depending on how much your crock pot will hold).

NOTE: I let mine cook in the crock pot for about two hours so all the flavors run together.

Also, I added worstershire sauce, lots of pepper, some salt and other seasonings to taste.

NUTRITIONAL INFORMATION

Serving Size: 10

Calories: 70.6

Total Fat: 0.7 g

Sodium: 623.6 mg

Total Carbs: 14.6 g

Dietary Fiber: 3.5 g

Protein: 2.8 g

Crock Pot Soup: Chicken, Vegetable and Rice Soup

Minutes to Prepare: *20*

Minutes to Cook: *240*

Number of Servings: *6*

Ingredients
4 Cups of College Inn Chicken Broth
12oz of Chicken (cut into bite size pieces)
2 cups of Frozen Mixed Vegetables
1 Cups of Brown rice (makes 3 ½ Cup cooked)

Directions

1. First, you put all the ingredients in the crock pot and leave it alone.
2. After which you put the rice and chicken in the crock pot uncooked, it will cook during the day.

NOTE: Cook times will vary depending on your crock pot (Mine cooked in 4 hours on high).

Enjoy!

NUTRITIONAL INFORMATION

Serving Size: 6

Calories: 207.0

Total Fat: 1.9 g

Sodium: 757.3 mg

Total Carbs: 31.3 g

Dietary Fiber: 2.7 g

Protein: 16.1 g

Diet Coke Chicken

Number of Servings: *4*

Ingredients
1 large onion (diced)
12 oz. diet coke
2 lbs. of chicken breast
1 large bell pepper (cut in strips)
1 cup of ketchup

Directions
1. First, you place everything in crock pot.
2. Then you cook on low for 6-8 hrs.
3. ENJOY!

NUTRITIONAL INFORMATION

Serving Size: 4

Calories: 92.8

Total Fat: 0.6 g

Sodium: 414.9 mg

Total Carbs: 13.5 g

Dietary Fiber: 1.1 g

Protein: 8.9 g

Beef Tips in Crockpot

Minutes to Prepare: *10*

Minutes to Cook: *360*

Number of Servings: *8*

Ingredients
2 envelopes of Lipton onion soup mix
1 cup of red wine (or better still beef broth)
4 cups of cooked rice
 2 lbs. of lean stew meat
2 (about 10 ½ oz.) cans 98% fat free mushroom soup
2 (about 8 oz.) cans sliced mushrooms (drained)

Directions

1. First, you mix all ingredients (except rice) in crockpot.
2. After which you cook for about 6-8 hours on low.
3. Then you serve over rice or noodles.

NUTRITIONAL INFORMATION

Serving Size: 8

Calories: 302.6

Total Fat: 5.9 g

Sodium: 442.9 mg

Total Carbs: 28.6 g

Dietary Fiber: 0.9 g

Protein: 28.6 g

Turkey breast meatloaf

Minutes to Prepare: *20*

Minutes to Cook: *360*

Number of Servings: *4*

Ingredients
¼ cup of bread crumbs
Onion flakes (to taste)
1 egg
1 lb. of ground turkey breast
Soy sauce, lite (to taste)
Garlic or garlic powder (to taste)
Black pepper (to taste)

Directions

1. First, you mix all ingredients together.
2. After which you form into a loaf in crock pot (lined with foil to make less of a mess)
3. Then you cook on low 6-8 hours.

NUTRITIONAL INFORMATION

Serving Size: 4

Calories: 199.1

Total Fat: 3.3 g

Sodium: 517.5 mg

Total Carbs: 12.0 g

Dietary Fiber: 1.4 g

Protein: 30.2 g

Pork Chops with Jalapeno-Pecan Cornbread Stuffing

Minutes to Prepare: *20*

Minutes to Cook: *300*

Number of Servings: 6

Ingredients

¾ cup of onion (chopped)
½ cup of coarsely chopped pecans
1 teaspoon of rubbed sage
1/8 teaspoon of black pepper
1 egg (lightly beaten)
6 boneless loin pork chops, 1 inch thick (about 1 ½ pounds)
¾ cup of celery (chopped)
¼ cup of chopped jalapeno's or green chilis
½ teaspoon of dried rosemary
4 cups of unseasoned cornbread stuffing mix
1 ¼ cups of reduced-sodium chicken broth

Directions

1. First, you trim excess fat from pork and discard.
2. After which you spray large skillet with nonstick cooking spray; heat over medium heat.
3. After that, you add pork; cook for about 10 minutes or until browned on all sides.
4. Then you remove; set aside.
5. Furthermore, you add onion, celery, pecans, jalapeno pepper, sage, rosemary and black pepper to skillet.
6. After that, you cook for about 5 minutes or until tender; set aside.
7. This is when you combine cornbread stuffing mix, vegetable mixture and broth in medium bowl; stir in egg.
8. In addition, you spoon stuffing mixture into slow cooker.
9. After which you arrange pork on top.
10. At this point, you cover and cook on Low about 5 hours or until pork is tender and barely pink in center.
11. Finally, you serve with vegetable salad, if desired.
12. Makes 6 servings.

NUTRITIONAL INFORMATION

Serving Size: 6

Calories: 536.2

Total Fat: 31.3 g

Sodium: 899.5 mg

Total Carbs: 33.1 g

Dietary Fiber: 5.6 g

Protein: 30.0 g

Turkey Stew

Minutes to Prepare: *15*

Minutes to Cook: *4*

Number of Servings: *10*

Ingredients
4 potatoes
½ cup of carrots
poultry seasonings
Turkey thigh
1 cup of raw cabbage shredded
1 small onion
8 cups of water

Directions

1. First, you put it all in Crock pot on high it will be done in about 4 hours.

NUTRITIONAL INFORMATION

Serving Size: 10

Calories: 97.8

Total Fat: 1.2 g

Sodium: 25.1 mg

Total Carbs: 16.5 g

Dietary Fiber: 1.8 g

Protein: 5.7 g

Homemade Refried Beans

Minutes to Prepare: *5*

Minutes to Cook: *300*

Number of Servings: *4*

Ingredients
4 teaspoons of BACON GREASE
2 cloves of GARLIC
1lb bag of DRY PINTO BEANS
1 teaspoon of SALT

Directions

1. First, you place beans in crock pot with WHOLE cloves garlic.
2. After which you cover with water; turn on HIGH and cook for about 4 to 5 hours or until beans are tender.
   (**NOTE:** KEEP EYE ON WATER LEVEL!! KEEP WATER COVERING BEANS)
3. After that, you drain "bean juice" in a bowl and slightly mash beans (**NOTE:** if you over mash beans they will be like paste/cement!).
4. At this point, you add bacon grease and salt; stir well.
5. Then you slowly add "bean juice" to reach desired consistency (**NOTE:** less if you like 'thick' beans, more if you want 'thinner' beans)

Remember that the serving sizes depend on what you're using them for i.e.: burritos, tacos, side dish...etc.... (I usually double recipe and save leftovers for kids burrito lunches!)

NUTRITIONAL INFORMATION **Serving Size:** 4

Calories: 228.3

Total Fat: 4.3 g

Sodium: 599.3 mg

Total Carbs: 69.2 g

Dietary Fiber: 43.8 g

Protein: 22.0 g

Cashew chicken

Minutes to Prepare: *15*

Minutes to Cook: *240*

Number of Servings: 6

Ingredients
2 tablespoons of soy sauce
1 ½ pounds of boneless, skinless, chicken breast
2 medium carrots, shredded (approx. one cup)
1- 8 oz. of can slice water chestnuts (drained)
Hot cooked brown rice (optional)
1- 10.75 oz. of Golden Mushroom can of soup (undiluted)
½ teaspoon of ground ginger
2 stalks of celery
1 cup of sliced mushrooms
½ cup of unsalted cashews

Directions

1. First you combine the soup, soy sauce, and ginger in a slow cooker.
2. After which you stir in chicken, celery, carrots and water chestnuts.
3. After that, you cover and cook on low setting for about 6-8 hours or high setting for 3-4 hours.
4. Then you stir in cashews into chicken mixture.
5. Finally, if desired serve over cooked rice.

NUTRITIONAL INFORMATION

Serving Size: 6

Calories: 273.9

Total Fat: 9.1 g

Sodium: 1,416.9 mg

Total Carbs: 16.4 g

Dietary Fiber: 2.6 g

Protein: 31.0 g

Chicken Enchilada Chili

Minutes to Prepare: *15*

Number of Servings: *12*

Ingredients

2 cups of shredded chicken

2 cans of diced tomatoes

2 cans of black or better still pinto beans

1 can of corn or better still 1 ½ cups frozen

3 celery stalks and 1 onion (diced)

1 can enchilada sauce

2 teaspoons of chili powder

1 teaspoon of cumin.
(**NOTE:** check enchilada sauce for hidden gluten)

Directions

Tip: Don't drain the beans or tomatoes.

1. First, you add everything to the crock pot for about 6-8 hours on low, closer to 8 hours if you're using anything frozen.

NUTRITIONAL INFORMATION

Serving Size: *12*

Calories: 154.4

Total Fat: 3.2 g

Sodium: 445.6 mg

Total Carbs: 16.8 g

Dietary Fiber: 3.9 g

Protein: 16.7 g

Crock Pot Stew with Brown Rice

Minutes to Prepare: *15*

Number of Servings: 6

Ingredients

1 lb. Beef chuck
Swanson Chicken Broth 99% Fat Free (396 grams)
3 cup Del Monte Petite Cut Diced Tomatoes
1 tablespoon of Oregano, ground
2 teaspoons of Garlic
Uncle Ben's Fast & Natural Whole Grain Instant Brown Rice (4 serving)

Directions

1. First, you mix all ingredients except for rice and put in crock pot.
2. After which you cook on high for 5 hours.
3. Serve over rice.

NUTRITIONAL INFORMATION

Serving Size: 6

Calories: 252.6

Total Fat: 5.5 g

Sodium: 836.5 mg

Total Carbs: 31.3 g

Dietary Fiber: 3.7 g

Protein: 18.9 g

Roxie's Calico Beans

Minutes to Prepare: *20*

Minutes to Cook: *90*

Number of Servings: *80*

Ingredients

1 lb. of bacon, crumbled
2 teaspoons of salt
2 teaspoons of mustard
2 (about 15-16 oz.) cans kidney beans
2 (about 20 oz.) cans Bush's Pork 'n Beans (**NOTE:** If you can't find Bush's you can substitute Van Kamp's but you have to add a little molasses.)
4 teaspoons of vinegar
1 lb. of lean ground beef
1 cup onion, chopped finely (or better still use minced onion)
1 ½ cup of brown sugar (packed)
1 cup of ketchup
1 (about 15-16 oz.) can butter beans
1 (about 15-16 oz.) can lima beans (drained)

Directions

1. First, you brown together ground beef, crumbled bacon, and onion.
2. After which you put mixture in the removable crock of a crock pot.
3. After that, you add the rest of the ingredients and stir well.
4. At this point, you bake in crock for 1 ½ hours at 325 degrees.
5. Then after baking keep warm in the regular part of the crock pot while serving.

(**NOTE:** Make sure you cook it all the way through before putting in the regular crock pot part.)

Tip: This BARELY fits in a 5-quart crock pot. To avoid spilling when baking, I suggest you use a 6-quart crock pot.

NUTRITIONAL INFORMATION

Serving Size: 1/2 cup

Number of Servings: 80

Calories: 82.7

Total Fat: 2.3 g

Sodium: 259.9 mg

Total Carbs: 13.6 g

Dietary Fiber: 2.3 g

Protein: 3.7 g

Apple Cinnamon Crock Pot Oatmeal

Minutes to Prepare: *10*

Number of Servings: *4*

Ingredients

Tips: For four servings, I suggest you use 3-4 qtr. Crock Pot.

1 teaspoon of cinnamon
2 cups of old-fashioned rolled oats
pinch salt
2 apples (peeled & sliced)
1/3 cup of brown sugar
4 cups of water

For two servings, I suggest you use 2 qtr. Crock Pot.

½ teaspoon of cinnamon
1 cup of old-fashioned rolled oats
dash salt
1 apple (peeled & sliced)
2 tablespoons plus 2 teaspoons of brown sugar
2 cups of water

Directions

NOTE: You will probably want to use a Crock Pot liner for this one (the brown sugar makes it a little messy).

1. First, you slice the apples and place in the bottom of the Crock Pot.
2. After which you add brown sugar and cinnamon over the apples, then stir until mixed.
3. After that, you pour the oats evenly over the apples.
4. At this point, you add water and salt.
5. Resist the urge to stir for it will mix itself when it is cooking.
6. Then you cook on low for about 8-9 hours (overnight).
7. Remember, you can turn it off when you get up in the morning and it will stay hot for a while, if you aren't ready for breakfast yet when you first get up.

8. Finally, stir well before serving, making sure to get the oats out of the bottom.

NUTRITIONAL INFORMATION

Serving Size: 4

Calories: 237.2

Total Fat: 3.3 g

Sodium: 4.8 mg

Total Carbs: 49.6 g

Dietary Fiber: 6.2 g

Protein: 5.2 g

Slow Cooker Chicken Tacos

Minutes to Prepare: *5*

Minutes to Cook: *480*

Number of Servings: *8*

Ingredients
1 (about 16 oz.) jar of salsa
1 package of taco seasoning
1 pound of boneless skinless chicken breasts

Directions

1. First, you cook in crock pot for about 8-10 hours on low.
2. After which you shred meat using forks, and serve on whole wheat tortillas with 2% cheddar cheese and non-fat refried beans. (Calories not included.)

NUTRITIONAL INFORMATION

Serving Size per recipe: 8

Calories: 91.0

Total Fat: 2.2 g

Sodium: 363.7 mg

Total Carbs: 4.8 g

Dietary Fiber: 1.0 g

Protein: 13.3 g

Crockpot Crazy Chicken

Minutes to Prepare: *10*

Number of Servings: 6

Ingredients

2 cups of salsa
1 teaspoon of cumin
½ tablespoon of mustard
6 boneless skinless chicken breasts
1 tablespoon of honey
1 teaspoon of chili powder
1 tablespoon of ketchup

Directions

1. First, you place chicken in the crock pot.
2. After which in a small bowl mix the remaining ingredients and pour over the chicken.
3. After that, you cover and cook on low for 6 to 8 hours.

Tips:

1. It is really good over rice or pasta (not included in nutritional info).
2. Make sure you serve each breast with about 1/3 cup of sauce.

NUTRITIONAL INFORMATION

Serving Size: Number of Servings: 6

Servings size Per Recipe: 6

Calories: 302.8

Total Fat: 3.1 g

Sodium: 843.9 mg

Total Carbs: 9.4 g

Dietary Fiber: 2.9 g

Protein: 54.7 g

Slow Cooker Pork Loin with Creamy Sauce

Minutes to Prepare: *10*

Minutes to Cook: *480*

Number of Servings: 8

Ingredients
One can 98% fat free cream of celery soup
1 medium onion (sliced)
½ teaspoon of black pepper
1 cup of water
2 ½ lbs. of pork tenderloin
1 can 98% fat free cream of mushroom soup
2 teaspoons of garlic (chopped)
2 tablespoons of soy sauce

Directions

1. First, you place the pork loin (may be frozen) into the crock pot.
2. After which you add the black pepper, soy sauce, garlic, onions, canned soups and water.
3. Then you cover and place on high for about 8 hours.
4. Makes 8 portions.

NUTRITIONAL INFORMATION

Number of Servings: 8

Servings per Recipe: 8

Amount per Serving

Calories: 276.2

Total Fat: 9.3 g

Sodium: 774.3 mg

Total Carbs: 8.1 g

Dietary Fiber: 1.0 g

Protein: 37.5 g

Low Sodium Mexican Chicken Stew in Slow Cooker

Minutes to Prepare: *10*

Minutes to Cook: *240*

Number of Servings: *12*

Ingredients
One Can Green Giant No Salt Added Whole Kernel Corn
One Can Nature's Promise Organic Black Beans
1 Onion (Diced)
One Can Tomato Sauce (with No Salt Added)
2 Teaspoons of Onion Powder
1 Teaspoon of Garlic Powder
1 Teaspoon of Ground Oregano
4 Frozen Chicken Breasts (or better still 20 Frozen Chicken Tenders)
1 Can Nature's Promise Organic Dark Kidney Beans
1 Can tomatoes (with No Salt Added, Diced)
1 Green Pepper (Diced)
2 Tablespoons of Chili Powder
2 Teaspoons of Ground Cumin
1 Teaspoon of Paprika

Directions

1. First, you place frozen chicken breasts (or tenders) in slow cooker.
2. After which you add remaining ingredients, and stir gently, leaving chicken on bottom.
3. After that, you cook on high for about 4-5 hours.
4. Remember, if you used chicken breasts, you can remove them and shred or chop them and add back to stew (I leave the chicken tenders in as they are, and mix the stew up well).
5. Sometimes I use to add small can of diced chili peppers to spice it up, but I did not include in this recipe because the sodium is deceiving. Remember that if you rinse them well, most of the salt rinses off, but I have no accurate nutritional info for this.
6. Finally, if you use fresh chicken, I suggest you cook on high for 3-4 hours.
7. Makes about 12 servings, 3/4 cup each.

NUTRITIONAL INFORMATION

Servings size Per Recipe: 12

Amount per Serving

Calories: 208.5

Total Fat: 1.6 g

Sodium: 162.3 mg

Total Carbs: 23.3 g

Dietary Fiber: 5.9 g

Protein: 25.6 g

Turkey & Veggie Meal

Minutes to Prepare: *20*

Minutes to Cook: *480*

Number of Servings: 6

Ingredients

2 cups of carrot (chopped)
1 ½ cups of yellow/crookneck squash (chopped)
3 cups of broccoli (chopped)
¾ cup of each red and orange bell peppers (chopped)
1 can College Inn Light & Fat Free Chicken Broth (50% less sodium)
1 teaspoon of sage, rosemary, thyme
1 cup of Heartland Whole Wheat Elbow Macaroni
2 cup of celery (chopped)
3 cups of white onion (chopped)
1 ½ cups of zucchini (chopped)
3 cups of spinach
1 cup of green bell pepper (chopped)
12 oz. cooked turkey (chopped)
1 cup of water
¼ teaspoon of coarse ground black pepper

Directions

1. First, you put everything except noodles in a 5 qt crockpot on low 6-8 hours.
2. After which you boil noodles 5 minutes, drain.
3. After that, you stir in to crockpot.
4. Then you turn to high 1-2 hours.

NUTRITIONAL INFORMATION

Serving Size: 2 cups

Number of Servings: 6

Calories: 253.6

Total Fat: 3.7 g

Sodium: 275.2 mg

Total Carbs: 33.4 g
Dietary Fiber: 7.4 g
Protein: 23.0 g

Chicken with Cheesy Mushroom Gravy

Tips:
1. Make sure you serve with a green salad on the side.
2. Serve over mashed potatoes.

Minutes to Prepare: *10*

Minutes to Cook: *60*

Number of Servings: *8*

Ingredients

1 cup of sliced fresh mushrooms
½ packet of Good Seasonings Italian dressing mix
4 chicken boneless, skinless chicken breasts
1 can of cream of mushroom soup
1 cup of shredded Cheddar cheese

Directions

1. First, you place the chicken in a glass baking dish.
2. After which you mix together the remaining ingredients and pour over chicken.
3. After that, you cover and bake at 350 for one hour, or until the chicken is fully cooked.

NOTE: makes 8 servings (Each serving is ½ chicken breast and 1/8 of the gravy).

NUTRITIONAL INFORMATION

Serving Size per recipe: 8

Amount per Serving

Calories: 236.6

Total Fat: 10.1 g

Sodium: 397.1 mg

Total Carbs: 3.5 g

Dietary Fiber: 0.1 g

Protein: 31.2 g

Low fat Cheeseburger Pie

NOTE: Remember that this lighter version of an old classic is made with lower-calorie baking mix and ground turkey instead of beef.

Minutes to Prepare: *15*

Minutes to Cook: *35*

Number of Servings: *8*

Ingredients
1 cup of fat-free cottage cheese
½ cup onion (chopped)
¾ cup of shredded reduced-fat Cheddar cheese
¼ cup of water
4 slices of tomato
1 pound extra lean ground turkey
1 egg
1 clove garlic (chopped)
1 tablespoons of Worcestershire sauce
¾ cup of Heart Smart Bisquick (mix only)

Directions

1. Meanwhile, you heat oven to 350.
2. After which you brown the turkey in a large skillet with the onions and garlic.
3. In the meantime, you combine the baking mix and water in a small bowl and roll the dough flat enough to cover a pie pan with rolling pin. (NOTE: You may have extra dough).
4. After that, you place the dough in the pie pan.
5. At this point, you add the Worcestershire sauce to the meat mixture.
6. Then in a medium bowl, mix the cottage cheese and egg.
7. This is when you pour the turkey mixture into pie pan, then top with the cottage cheese mixture and the cheese.
8. Finally, you top with the tomatoes and bake for about 30-40 minutes.

NUTRITIONAL INFORMATION

Serving Size per Recipe: 8

Calories: 166.5

Total Fat: 4.5 g

Sodium: 359.4 mg

Total Carbs: 10.7 g

Dietary Fiber: 0.3 g

Protein: 21.2 g

Slow-Cooker Salsa Chicken

Number of Servings: 6

Ingredients

1 cup of salsa
½ cup of reduced fat sour cream
4 boneless, skinless chicken breasts
1 package of reduced sodium taco seasoning
1 can of reduced fat cream of mushroom soup (condensed)

Directions

1. First, you add chicken to slow cooker.
   After which you sprinkle taco seasoning over chicken.
2. After that, you pour salsa and soup over chicken.
3. Then you cook on low for about 6 to 8 hours.
4. At this point, you remove from heat and stir in sour cream.
5. Finally, you serve with rice.

   ### Tips:

1. Feel free to use half the packet of taco seasoning (I have started doing this to reduce sodium content myself)
2. Remember, some slow cookers cook faster than others. Mine is a true slow cooker (have had it over 10 years.) The newer ones cook a bit faster and I suggest that you adjust your cooking time based on that!

NUTRITIONAL INFORMATION

Serving Size per Recipe: 6

Amount per Serving

Calories: 197.2

Total Fat: 6.8 g

Sodium: 464.2 mg

Total Carbs: 6.7 g

Dietary Fiber: 0.9 g

Protein: 26.3 g

Crock Pot Sour Cream and Onion Chicken

Tip:

1. Remember, this crock pot meal of baked chicken in a creamy onion sauce is fast, easy to prepare and tastes great.
2. This is one of the easiest meals to put together and has become a family favorite.
3. However, it is very creamy and goes well with wild rice or potatoes.
4. Remember this recipe doubles nicely for larger servings.

Minutes to Prepare: *30*

Minutes to Cook: *320*

Number of Servings: *4*

Ingredients

1 (12 oz.) can of low fat cream of mushroom soup
1 ½ cups of water
1 packet of onion soup mix
4 chicken breast halves
½ cup of fat free sour cream

Directions

1. First, you place thawed chicken into crock pot or slow cooker.
2. Then in a medium bowl, you mix all the other ingredients together.
3. After that, you pour mixture of chicken and cover.
4. At this point, you cook at low setting for about 6-8 hours or higher setting for 4-6 hours.

NUTRITIONAL INFORMATION

Number of Servings: 4

Servings per Recipe: 4

Amount per Serving

Calories: 336.0

Total Fat: 7.1 g

Sodium: 573.3 mg

Total Carbs: 7.8 g

Dietary Fiber: 0.5 g

Protein: 56.0 g

Thai Chicken with Peanut Sauce

Minutes to Prepare: *10*

Minutes to Cook: *240*

Number of Servings: 6

Ingredients
1 bottle of Peanut Sauce
16oz. of peeled baby carrots
3 Boneless, Skinless Chicken breasts (cut in half)
1 cup of Coconut milk

Directions
1. First, you place the bag of carrots in bottom of slow cooker.
2. After which you place chicken over that.
3. Then you pour sauce on top.
4. At this point, you cook on low for 8 to 10 hours or on high for about 4 to 6 hours.
5. Furthermore, you add 1 cup of coconut milk and stir.
6. Finally, you serve over brown rice

NUTRITIONAL INFORMATION

Number of Servings: 6

Servings per Recipe: 6

Amount per Serving

Calories: 287.1

Total Fat: 14.1 g

Sodium: 522.2 mg

Total Carbs: 8.5 g

Dietary Fiber: 0.0 g

Protein: 29.9 g

Cowboy Chicken

Number of Servings: 6

Ingredients

One jar (about 2 cups) your favorite Salsa (mild, medium, or hot)
1 Tablespoon of Brown Mustard or better still Dijon Mustard
6 - Chicken Breast halves (no skin)
1-2 Tablespoons of Brown Sugar

Directions

1. First, you place chicken in crock pot or casserole dish.
2. After which you mix all other ingredients in bowl and pour over chicken.
3. Then you cook in crock pot on low for about 6 hours, or bake in 375f oven for about 1 hour.

NOTE: the sauce is delicious over rice, scooped up with baked tortilla chips, or even served over steamed veggies.

NUTRITIONAL INFORMATION

Number of Servings: 6

Servings per Recipe: 6

Amount per Serving

Calories: 172.8

Total Fat: 1.7 g

Sodium: 489.4 mg

Total Carbs: 9.6 g

Dietary Fiber: 1.4 g

Protein: 28.3 g

Stacey's Crock-pot Chicken and Dumplings

Minutes to Prepare: *10*

Minutes to Cook: *360*

Number of Servings: *10*

Ingredients
1 can of Campbell's Cream of Chicken Soup (98% fat free)
2 soup cans of water
1 small onion
Salt and pepper to taste
½ lb. of Chicken Breast (raw)
1 can of Healthy Request Cream of Mushroom Soup
½ bag of frozen Mixed Vegetables (about 1lb bag)
1 tablespoon of minced garlic
1 can of Biscuit, plain or buttermilk, 8 biscuits

Directions

1. First, you spray crock-pot with Pam and cut chicken breasts into halves, place chicken on the bottom of the crock-pot.
2. After which you dice up onion and mince garlic; add to crock-pot along with cream of chicken and mushroom soup, 2 soup cans of water, frozen mixed vegetables, mix together.
3. Then you cook on high for about 6-8 hours, 2 hours before serving, cut biscuits in strips or into quarters, set on top of soup mixture or mix everything together.

NOTE: If you want more of a doughy noodle, I suggest you stir biscuits into the mixture.

Number of Servings: 10

Crock-pot Chicken Ragu (slow cooker)

Tip:

This is a very easy recipe that satisfies my craving for Chicken Parmesan.

Minutes to Prepare: *5*

Minutes to Cook: *300*

Number of Servings: *6*

Ingredients
One jar Ragu Spaghetti Sauce (90 calories per serving)
1 ½ cup Kraft Shredded Mozzarella Cheese
18 oz. Boneless, Skinless Chicken Breast

Directions

1. First, you place chicken in crock-pot (NOTE: I use "Tender Bird" brand frozen chicken tenders (1/2 of 3 lb. bag) and I do not thaw).
2. After which you spoon Ragu sauce over the chicken and cook on low for 6-8 hours.
3. Then about 15 minutes before serving, sprinkle shredded cheese over the chicken and sauce.
4. Finally, you cover and let cheese melt (I serve this with steamed broccoli and a salad).

    Makes 6 servings.

NUTRITIONAL INFORMATION

Number of Servings: 6

Servings per Recipe: 6

Amount per Serving

Calories: 263.5

Total Fat: 9.6 g

Sodium: 825.3 mg

Total Carbs: 11.0 g

Dietary Fiber: 2.0 g

Protein: 29.6 g

Slow Cooker Barbecue Orange Chicken

Minutes to Prepare: *10*

Minutes to Cook: *300*

Number of Servings: *3*

Ingredients
1/3 cup of sugar free orange marmalade
1/3 cup of barbecue sauce
3 boneless, skinless, chicken thighs
1/3 cup of flour
2 tablespoons of lite soy sauce

Directions

1. First, you place chicken in slow cooker.
2. After which you spoon flour over chicken and mix until coated.
3. After that, you mix barbecue sauce, marmalade, and soy sauce and pour over chicken.
4. Then you cook on low for about 4-6 hours.

NUTRITIONAL INFORMATION

Number of Servings: 3

Servings per Recipe: 3

Amount per Serving

Calories: 221.3

Total Fat: 2.8 g

Sodium: 802.5 mg

Total Carbs: 33.1 g

Dietary Fiber: 0.6 g

Protein: 15.6 g

Crock Pot Chicken Cacciatore (Low Sodium)

TIPS:

1. Remember, this is a large recipe for batch cooking and freezes great!
2. The recipe is calculated using boneless, skinless chicken thighs; to reduce the fat, I suggest you use boneless, skinless breasts instead.
3. Low sodium at 114mg per serving.

Minutes to Prepare: *15*

Minutes to Cook: *720*

Number of Servings: *18*

Ingredients
2 (15oz) cans Hunt's Tomato Sauce (with no salt added)
2 Medium Onions (chopped)
2 tablespoons of Basil
9 teaspoons of Splenda granulated
6lbs Boneless Skinless Chicken Thigh
2 cups of chopped Green Peppers (bell peppers)
2 (14.5oz) cans Del Monte Diced Tomatoes (with No Salt Added
2 tablespoons of dried Parsley (dried)
1 tablespoon of Oregano

Directions

1. First, you pour a thin layer of tomato sauce in the bottom of the crock pot, then arrange boneless, skinless chicken thighs or breasts in a single layer.
2. After which you chop onion and bell pepper and layer over chicken.
3. After that, you mix remaining tomato sauce, diced tomatoes, ½ cup water, and spices in a bowl and pour in an even layer across the top, covering well.
4. Then you cook on low for about 10-12 hours.
5. When done cooking, you break up the chicken thighs into with a spatula and mix well.
6. It makes 18 servings, approximately 2/3 cup per serving.

NUTRITIONAL INFORMATION

Number of Servings: 18

Servings per Recipe: 18

Amount per Serving

Calories: 281.9

Total Fat: 13.2 g

Sodium: 114.1 mg

Total Carbs: 8.8 g

Dietary Fiber: 2.2 g

Protein: 35.1 g

Slow Cooker Garlic Tomato Chicken

Number of Servings: 6

Ingredients

2 cups of Lima Beans (dry)
3 cloves Garlic (mashed)
1 teaspoon of Cumin
½ teaspoon of Salt
1 cup of Water (or better still enough to make slow cooker halfway full)
2 Chicken Breasts (4 halves)
1 cup of Tomato Sauce
1 teaspoon of Allspice
1 teaspoon of Black Pepper
1 teaspoon of Oregano
(**NOTE:** That's just my taste for spices, alter them to your taste).

Directions

1. First, you pour dry Lima Beans, tomato sauce, and water into Slow Cooker.
2. After which you brown chicken over medium heat.
3. After that, you put chicken into Slow Cooker and let cook for 5-6 hours on low.
4. At this point, you add spices and garlic in the last hour or two of cooking (still on low).

NOTE: at this point, it might need some mixing and a little more water to keep it from burning.

5. Then after letting it cook for 8-ish hours, eat it up! (Tastes great over a bed of brown rice).

NUTRITIONAL INFORMATION

Number of Servings: 6

Servings per Recipe: 6

Amount per Serving

Calories: 182.1

Total Fat: 1.5 g

Sodium: 462.4 mg

Total Carbs: 18.4 g

Dietary Fiber: 5.6 g

Protein: 23.8 g

Pork and Potatoes in Mustard Sauce

TIPS:

This is a great recipe to throw in the slow cooker before work and it will be ready for you when you get home from work.

Number of Servings: 6

Ingredients

1-10 ¾ oz. fat free cream of mushroom soup
¼ cup of Dijon mustard
1-2 cloves of garlic (minced)
1 onion (sliced)
6 (4-oz) pork loin chops
¼ cup of chicken broth
½ teaspoon of dried thyme
Salt and pepper to taste
6 medium potatoes (sliced thin)

Directions

1. First, you combine soup, broth, mustard, potatoes, onions and garlic in a slow cooker.
2. After which you sprinkle salt, pepper and thyme on pork and put on top of mixture.
3. Then you cook on low for 8 hours or high for about 4-6 hours.

NUTRITIONAL INFORMATION

Number of Servings: 6

Servings per Recipe: 6

Amount per Serving

Calories: 439.1

Total Fat: 11.5 g

Sodium: 554.7 mg

Total Carbs: 43.6 g

Dietary Fiber: 5.5 g

Protein: 36.3 g

Easy Slow Cooker Lemony Garlic Chicken Breast

Number of Servings: 6

Ingredients

¼ teaspoon of black pepper
1 tablespoon of olive oil
3 tablespoons of lemon juice
1 teaspoon of parsley
1 teaspoon of oregano
2 lbs. of boneless, skinless chicken breasts (six halves)
¼ cup of water
2 teaspoons of minced garlic
1 teaspoon of chicken bouillon granules

Directions

1. First, you mix oregano and pepper and sprinkle evenly over chicken pieces.
2. After which in a large non-stick skillet, using medium heat, brown chicken evenly on both sides in olive oil.
3. After that, you mix remaining ingredients and pour over chicken, bringing mixture to a gentle boil.
4. Then you pour skillet contents into slow cooker, cover, and cook on low for 6 hours (3 hours on high).
5. Note that chicken is very tasty served on a bed of brown rice with steamed carrots!

NUTRITIONAL INFORMATION

Servings per Recipe: 6

Amount per Serving

Calories: 167.8

Total Fat: 5.6 g

Sodium: 127.6 mg

Total Carbs: 0.9 g

Dietary Fiber: 0.2 g

Protein: 27.0 g

Slow-Cooker Chicken Paprikash

Tips:

This recipe is great served over mashed potatoes, spaetzle, or broad egg noodles.

Minutes to Prepare: *15*

Minutes to Cook: *480*

Number of Servings: *6*

Ingredients

2 pounds of skinless, boneless chicken breast (cut into ½ -inch strips)
1 ¼ cups of fat-free, less-sodium chicken broth
½ cup of shredded carrot
4 cloves of minced garlic
1 teaspoon of black pepper
1 ¼ cups of reduced-fat sour cream
3 tablespoons of all-purpose flour
1 large onion (chopped)
1 large red bell pepper (chopped)
2 tablespoons of Hungarian sweet paprika
1 teaspoon of salt
1 (8-ounce) package pre-sliced mushrooms

Directions

1. First, you combine flour and chicken in a large Ziploc bag; toss well, making sure chicken is coated.
2. After which you add chicken mixture and remaining ingredients (except sour cream) to an electric slow cooker.
3. After that, you cover and cook on low for 8 hours.
4. Then you stir in sour cream just before serving (makes 6 1-cup servings).

   Number of Servings: 6

NUTRITIONAL INFORMATION

Servings per Recipe: 6

Amount per Serving

Calories: 298.7

Total Fat: 8.7 g

Sodium: 628.5 mg

Total Carbs: 15.5 g

Dietary Fiber: 3.2 g

Protein: 39.5 g

Crock pot macaroni and cheese

Minutes to Prepare: *15*

Minutes to Cook: *120*

Number of Servings: 6

Ingredients
1 tablespoon of smart balance omega buttery spread melted (not light)
3 cups of shredded 2% cheddar cheese
¼ teaspoon of pepper
3 cups of cooked macaroni
2 cups of evaporated milk
1 teaspoon of salt

Directions

1. First, you add all ingredients into slow cooker.
2. Then you cook on high for 2-3 hours stirring twice.

    Note: I used regular evaporated milk in this recipe because that's all I had.

NUTRITIONAL INFORMATION

Number of Servings: 6

Servings per Recipe: 6

Amount per Serving

Calories: 401.4

Total Fat: 18.8 g

Sodium: 1,008.5 mg

Total Carbs: 31.8 g

Dietary Fiber: 1.1 g

Protein: 23.8 g

Slow Cooked Chicken Breast with Peppers

Number of Servings: *1*

Ingredients

1 teaspoon of pepper, black
1 small onion (chopped)
1 cup of chicken broth (fat free)
1 chicken breast (no skin)
1 cup of sweet peppers or better still hot peppers
1 cup of whole mushrooms (or better still sliced)

Directions

1. First, you place all ingredients in a slow cooker.
2. After which you cook until done, cooking time will be different for each slow cooker; takes 4 to 6 hours.

NUTRITIONAL INFORMATION

Number of Servings: 1

Servings per Recipe: 1

Amount per Serving

Calories: 168.4

Total Fat: 2.0 g

Sodium: 546.5 mg

Total Carbs: 18.2 g

Dietary Fiber: 5.4 g

Protein: 22.3 g

Maple Flavored Barbeque Chicken - Crock Pot

Number of Servings: *4*

Ingredients

1 cup of ketchup
2 Tablespoons of prepared mustard
2 teaspoons of lemon juice
¼ teaspoon of garlic powder
4 boneless chicken breasts
½ cup of maple syrup
2 Tablespoons of Worcestershire sauce
½ teaspoon of chili powder

Directions

1. First, you combine all ingredients in crockpot.
2. After which you cover and cook on LOW for about 7-8 hours.
3. Then you remove chicken, shred and return to pot. (NOTE: Good over rice or on a bun)

NUTRITIONAL INFORMATION

Number of Servings: 4

Servings per Recipe: 4

Amount per Serving

Calories: 689.9

Total Fat: 3.6 g

Sodium: 1,136.2 mg

Total Carbs: 101.9 g

Dietary Fiber: 0.4 g

Protein: 56.6 g

Pork Chops for the Slow Cooker

Minutes to Prepare: *5*

Minutes to Cook: *360*

Number of Servings: *5*

Ingredients

3 tablespoons and 1 teaspoon of brown sugar
1/3 cup and 1 tablespoon and 1 teaspoon soy sauce
Salt and pepper to taste
5 boneless pork chops
¾ teaspoons of ground ginger
3 tablespoons and 1 teaspoon ketchup
1-2/3 cloves garlic (crushed)

Directions

1. First, you place pork chops in slow cooker.
2. After which you combine remaining ingredients and pour over pork chops.

Then you cook on Low setting for 6 hours, until internal temperature of pork has reached 160 degrees F (70 degrees C).

NUTRITIONAL INFORMATION

Number of Servings: 5

Servings per Recipe: 5

Amount per Serving

Calories: 392.5

Total Fat: 15.4 g

Sodium: 1,362.3 mg

Total Carbs: 10.8 g

Dietary Fiber: 0.3 g

Protein: 48.4 g

Slow cooker beef barley vegetable soup

Tips:

This recipe is a hearty soup full of vegetables

Minutes to Prepare: *10*

Minutes to Cook: *480*

Number of Servings: *8*

Ingredients
4 celery stalks (chopped)
1 can diced tomatoes (undrained)
5 Cups beef broth
1 Cup quick cooking barley
1 pound of beef stew meat (cubed)
4 carrots (chopped)
2 Tablespoons of tomato paste
1 Tablespoon of season salt

Directions

1. First, you add all ingredients except barley to slow cooker.
2. After which you cook on medium for 6-8 hours or until vegetables are tender.
3. After that, you cook barley according to package directions.
4. Then you add to soup and serve.

NUTRITIONAL INFORMATION

Number of Servings: 8

Servings per Recipe: 8

Amount per Serving

Calories: 180.4

Total Fat: 5.1 g

Sodium: 720.2 mg

Total Carbs: 13.0 g

Dietary Fiber: 3.1 g

Protein: 20.5 g

Slow Cooker Honey Mustard Chicken

Tips:

1. **Note** that this slow cooker recipe requires no pre-cooking, and it yields a sweet, caramelized glaze and tender chicken.
2. Remember that the Dijon and country-style mustards thicken the sauce.
3. However, if you use yellow mustard, you might have to thicken the sauce in the last 30 minutes of cooking with one tablespoon of water mixed with 2 teaspoons of cornstarch.

Minutes to Prepare: *15*

Minutes to Cook: *360*

Number of Servings: *4*

Ingredients

1 pound boneless, skinless chicken breasts (sliced into 1-inch strips)

Ingredients for the Sauce:
3 garlic cloves (sliced)
¼ cup of Dijon mustard
2 teaspoons of tomato paste
2 teaspoons of olive oil
Pinch cayenne pepper
1 large onion, sliced (about 1 ½ cups)
2 tablespoons of honey
1 tablespoon of country-style (coarse-grain) mustard
1 tablespoon of red wine vinegar
1 teaspoon of thyme
¼ teaspoon of black pepper
2 green onions, sliced on an angle, for garnish (it is optional)

Directions

1. First, you coat the slow cooker with cooking spray.
2. After which you place the chicken in the slow cooker.
3. After that, you add the sauce ingredients along with ½ cup water and stir to combine.

4. Then you cover and cook on low for 6-8 hours, until the chicken reaches an internal temperature of 165 degrees F.
5. Finally, you garnish with green onions before serving, if desired.

NUTRITIONAL INFORMATION

Serving Size: Makes 4 servings (1/2 cup)

Servings per Recipe: 4

Amount per Serving

Calories: 199.6

Total Fat: 4.9 g

Sodium: 373.4 mg

Total Carbs: 16.0 g

Dietary Fiber: 1.4 g

Protein: 24.8 g

Slow Cooker Bourbon Street Chicken

Tips:

1. Note that this is New Orleans-style chicken made with shredded dark meat in a lightly sweet sauce.
2. This recipe is delicious served over brown rice (Kids love it, too).

Minutes to Prepare: *15*

Minutes to Cook: *480*

Number of Servings: 6

Ingredients

1 clove garlic, chopped (or 1 tablespoon of granulated garlic)
¼ cup of apple juice
2 tablespoons of ketchup
1/8 cup of soy sauce
6 frozen chicken thighs
¼ teaspoon of ground ginger
¼ cup of packed light brown sugar
1 tablespoon of cider vinegar
½ cup of water

Directions

1. First, you place frozen chicken thighs on bottom of crock pot.
2. After which you combine remaining ingredients and pour over chicken.
3. After that, you cook 8 hours on low, then shred chicken in the slow cooker to a "pulled pork" consistency.
4. Then you ladle over a bowl of brown rice or place atop a whole-grain bun. (It not included in Nutrition Facts).

NOTE: green onion garnish and a side salad make it a meal.

NUTRITIONAL INFORMATION

Serving Size: Makes six servings.

Servings per Recipe: 6

Amount per Serving

Calories: 168.4

Total Fat: 4.0 g

Sodium: 537.1 mg

Total Carbs: 15.5 g

Dietary Fiber: 0.1 g

Protein: 19.5 g

Black Bean Chicken

Number of Servings: 6

Ingredients
16 ounces jarred salsa
1 pound of boneless, skinless chicken breasts
2 cans black beans
½ cup of brown rice (uncooked)

Directions

1. First, you place chicken breasts in slow cooker.
2. After which you pour beans, rice and salsa over chicken.
3. Then you cook on low for about 8-10 hours and serve.

Slow Cooker Pork Chop Dinner

Tips

Remember, you can change up the herb blend as desired.
Our blend contained dried parsley, oregano, basil, and thyme.

Minutes to Prepare: *25*

Minutes to Cook: *300*

Number of Servings: *4*

Ingredients

1 tablespoon of olive oil
2 (about 8 ounces) cups of sliced mushrooms
1 ½ cups of low-sodium chicken stock
¼ teaspoon of black pepper
4 cups of fresh green beans, trimmed (about 12 ounces)
4 (about 4-ounce) boneless top loin pork chops
1 medium white or yellow onion, sliced (about 1 cup)
1 tablespoon of flour
2 teaspoons of no salt Italian seasoning blend
1 pound redskin potatoes, quartered (about 8 potatoes)

Directions

1. First, you place a large skillet over medium-high heat, then coat with cooking spray.
2. After which you add the pork and cook two minutes per side.
3. After that, you set the pork chops aside, then return the skillet to the heat.
4. Then you add the oil, then the onions.
5. At this point, you cook for three minutes, stirring occasionally.
6. Furthermore, you add the mushrooms and cook another two minutes, until the mushrooms are soft and starting to brown.
7. After that, you stir in the flour and cook for one minute, then slowly pour in the stock.
8. This is when you stir constantly for three minutes, until the sauce thickens.
9. After which you add the seasoning blend and pepper, then turn off the heat.
10. In addition, you place the potatoes in the bottom of the slow cooker.
11. Then you top with the pork, then the onion-mushroom mixture.

12. Finally, you cover and cook on low for five to six hours.
13. Add the green beans when it is about 15 minutes before you're ready to eat.
14. Cook until tender and serve immediately.

NUTRITIONAL INFORMATION

Servings size Per Recipe: 4

Amount per Serving

Calories: 418.6

Total Fat: 19.8 g

Sodium: 79.5 mg

Total Carbs: 37.3 g

Dietary Fiber: 6.6 g

Protein: 25.8 g

Slow Cooker Rotisserie Chicken

TIPS:

1. Remember that those rotisserie chickens from the supermarket are a busy cook's best friend.
2. When you have time to plan ahead, I suggest you make your own in your slow cooker!
3. Remember, lifting the whole chicken up off the bottom of the slow cooker insert will keep air flowing all around the bird and let most of the fat fall to the bottom of the slow cooker.
4. However, you may not need a knife to cut this chicken once cooked-- the meat will almost fall off the bone.
5. Feel free to use other herbs and spices, if you prefer.

Minutes to Prepare: *10*

Minutes to Cook: *240*

Number of Servings: *4*

Ingredients

1 (about 4 ½ pounds) whole chicken

¼ teaspoon of black pepper

1 teaspoon of dried thyme

1 lemon (cut in half)

Directions

1. First, you place an inverted shallow ceramic dish (one that is oven-proof) into the bottom of your slow cooker insert.
2. (**NOTE:** your chicken should be able to fit on top and still allow the lid to close tightly).
3. After which in a small dish, squeeze the juice from half the lemon, then stir in the thyme and pepper.
4. After that, starting at the tail end of the bird (the end where the legs are), slide your fingers between the breast and the skin.
5. Then you loosen the skin from the flesh as you work your way to the neck end.

6. Furthermore, once the skin is loosened from the breast, cut it off and removing any fat, using kitchen shears if necessary.
7. After that, you continue the process with the skin over the legs (discard the skin).
8. At this point, you place the remaining ½ lemon into the cavity of the chicken, along with ¼ of the herbed lemon juice.
9. In addition, you cross the legs of the chicken, then tie them together with cotton kitchen string.
10. After which you place the chicken in the slow cooker, a top the inverted dish.
11. After that, you coat the top of the chicken with cooking spray.
12. Then you spoon the remaining herb mixture over the top and sides of the chicken.
13. This is when you cover and set on low.
14. At this point, you cook at least 4 but up to 8 hours, until temperature of the inner part of the chicken thigh reaches 170 degrees.
15. Finally, you transfer chicken to cutting board, let rest for 15 minutes, and then remove the meat from the bones.

Serving Size:

1. 1 (4 ½) pound chicken yields almost 10 ounces cooked dark meat and 16 ounces cooked white meat.
2. It approximately 2 ounces dark meat and 4 ounces of white meat per serving.

NUTRITIONAL INFORMATION

Servings per Recipe: 4

Amount per Serving

Calories: 277.8

Total Fat: 11.9 g

Sodium: 283.6 mg

Total Carbs: 2.9 g

Dietary Fiber: 1.2 g

Protein: 41.7 g

Slow Cooker Kentucky Burgoo

Minutes to Prepare: *15*

Minutes to Cook: *360*

Number of Servings: *8*

Ingredients

8 ounces boneless chicken breast (fat removed)
2 (about 1 cup) medium carrots, diced
2 garlic cloves (chopped)
½ teaspoon of black pepper
½ teaspoon of thyme, dried
2 cups of homemade chicken stock
1 cup of frozen lima beans
hot sauce to taste
16 ounces extra lean pork tenderloin, fat and silver skin removed (yields about 14 ounces)
3 (about 1 1/2 cups) medium yellow onions, chopped
3 (about 1 cup) stalks celery, diced
One 14.5-ounce can no salt added diced tomatoes
¼ teaspoon of red pepper flakes
1 bay leaf
1 large sweet potato (diced into 1 inch cubes)
1 cup of frozen corn
1 tablespoon of cornstarch

Tips

If you don't like sweet potatoes, I suggest you try redskin potatoes instead.

Directions

1. First, you dice the pork and chicken into 3/4 inch cubes.
2. After which you add the meats, onions, carrots, celery, garlic, tomatoes, spices, and stock to a slow cooker.

3. After that, you stir to combine, layer the sweet potatoes on top, then cover and cook on low for 5-6 hours.
4. Then after 5-6 hours, add the lima beans and corn, stir and cook for another 30 minute to an hour.
5. At this point, you combine the cornstarch with ¼ cup water, then add to the stew.
6. Stir and cook for about 10 more minutes with the lid off before serving.
7. Make sure you serve with hot sauce to taste.

Serves size 8 (1 ¼ cups per serving)

NUTRITIONAL INFORMATION

Servings per Recipe: 8

Amount per Serving

Calories: 192.9

Total Fat: 2.1 g

Sodium: 94.7 mg

Total Carbs: 22.5 g

Dietary Fiber: 4.9 g

Protein: 21.6 g

Slow Cooker Beef Roast with Vegetables

1. **NOTE: you should t**ry using an English Cut Beef Roast, because it is economical and flavorful.
2. Remember, this cut of meat comes from the shoulder or neck area of the animal.

Minutes to Prepare: *10*

Minutes to Cook: *480*

Number of Servings: *6*

Ingredients

1 ½ cups of carrots, baby peeled
1 large parsnip (peeled and chopped)
5 red skin new potatoes (washed and quartered)
1 teaspoon of black pepper
1 tablespoon of all-purpose flour
1 teaspoon of thyme (dried)
1 bay leaf (whole)
1 onion (chopped)
2 cloves garlic (sliced in half)
1 rutabaga (peeled and chopped)
2 ½ pounds beef roast, English or better still Cross Rib cut
½ teaspoon of salt
15 ounces salt-free pureed tomatoes
½ teaspoon of rosemary (dried)

Directions

1. First, you place all vegetables in the bottom of a slow cooker.
2. After which you season both sides of the meat with black pepper and salt.
3. Meanwhile, you heat a large sauté pan to moderately high heat; once hot spray pan with pan spray.
4. After that, you lightly flour beef then sear meat on all sides for about 3-4 minutes per side.
5. Then you place meat over vegetables.
6. At this point, you combine tomato sauce and seasonings.
7. Furthermore, you pour over meat and set slow cooker on low.

8. Finally, you cook for about 8-9 hours after which you remove meat and shred (Makes 6 servings. 4 ounces of cooked meat and 1 cup vegetables)

NUTRITIONAL INFORMATION

Servings per Recipe: 6

Amount per Serving

Calories: 349.8

Total Fat: 9.3 g

Sodium: 342.3 mg

Total Carbs: 21.1 g

Dietary Fiber: 4.2 g

Protein: 43.9 g

Slow Cooker Marinara Chicken and Vegetables

Tips:

In the morning, you throw all the ingredients for this simple recipe in the slow cooker. Have in mind that a hearty and healthy dinner will be waiting for you when you get home!

Minutes to Prepare: *5*

Minutes to Cook: *360*

Number of Servings: *8*

Ingredients

4 cloves garlic (peeled and crushed)
4 (about 1 cup) medium ribs celery, diced
1 bell pepper (cored, seeded, and diced)
1 teaspoon of dried thyme
2 pounds boneless, skinless chicken breasts
4 tomatoes, chopped or better still one 14 ½ -ounce can low-sodium tomatoes, drained
2 (2 cups) small zucchini, diced
One 18-ounce jar low-sodium marinara sauce
1 teaspoon of dried basil

Directions

1. First, you place the chicken in the slow cooker.
2. After which you add the garlic, tomatoes, celery, zucchini, and pepper.
3. After that, you pour the marinara sauce over all, and sprinkle the basil and thyme on top.
4. Then you set the slow cooker on low and cook for 6 to 7 hours.
5. Finally, before serving, shred the chicken with a fork.

NUTRITIONAL INFORMATION

Servings per Recipe: 8

Amount per Serving

Calories: 176.8

Total Fat: 3.7 g

Sodium: 129.4 mg

Total Carbs: 7.9 g

Dietary Fiber: 1.8 g

Protein: 26.8 g

Slow Cooker Creamy Paprika Pork

Tips:

Feel free to serve this comforting Hungarian classic with steamed brown rice and spinach or over whole-wheat egg noodles.

Minutes to Prepare: *15*

Minutes to Cook: *360*

Number of Servings: *4*

Ingredients

2 (about 1 ½ cups) large white or yellow onions, sliced
2 tablespoons of Hungarian or better still sweet paprika
1 bay leaf
2 (chopped) tablespoons of parsley
16 (cut into ½ inch cubes) ounces pork tenderloin, trimmed of fat
2 cloves garlic (minced)
1/8 teaspoon of cayenne pepper
1 ½ cups of homemade chicken stock
½ cup of fat-free plain Greek yogurt

Directions

1. First, you coat a large skillet with cooking spray and place over medium heat.
2. After which you add the pork and cook for three to four minutes, until the pork is no longer pink.
3. After that, you transfer the pork to a slow cooker, then return the pan to the heat.
4. Then you coat with more cooking spray, then add the onions and garlic.
5. At this point, you cook for three minutes, stirring occasionally.
6. Furthermore, you stir in the paprika and cayenne, along with ¼ cup stock.
7. After which you stir vigorously to scrape up any cooked-on bits from the bottom of the pan, then pour everything into the slow cooker, along with the rest of the stock and the bay leaf.
8. This is when you cook on low for five to seven hours, until the pork is tender.
9. Finally, you turn off heat, remove the bay leaf, and slowly stir in yogurt and parsley.

10. Make sure you serve immediately.

Serves size 4 (3/4 cup per portion)

NUTRITIONAL INFORMATION

Servings per Recipe: 4

Amount per Serving

Calories: 211.2

Total Fat: 4.5 g

Cholesterol: 82.6 mg

Sodium: 77.8 mg

Total Carbs: 7.7 g

Dietary Fiber: 2.2 g

Protein: 34.4 g

BONUS RECIPE

Crock Pot Salmon Fillets and Vegetables

NUTRITIONAL INFORMATION

Serving Size: Per Serving (1/2 fish and vegetables):

190 calories

6.8 g fat

16.4 g carbs

2.5 g fiber

16.7 g protein

Ingredients

1 package of frozen Asian stir fry vegetable blend (about 12 to 16 ounces)

2 tablespoons of soy sauce

1 teaspoon of sesame seeds (it is optional)

10 ounces of salmon fillets

Salt and Pepper

2 tablespoons of honey

2 tablespoons of lemon juice

Directions:

(**NOTE:** I used my 1-1/2-Quart crock pot in preparing this recipe).

1. First, you dump the frozen vegetables in the slow cooker.
2. After which you season the salmon with salt and pepper to taste.
3. After that, you place salmon on top of the vegetables.
4. At this point, you mix together the soy sauce, honey and lemon juice and drizzle over the salmon.
5. Then you drizzle with sesame seeds, if using.
6. Furthermore, you cover and cook on LOW for about 2 to 3 hours, until the salmon is done to your liking.
7. Feel free to serve with brown rice, if desired.
8. Finally, you drizzle everything with the sauce from the slow cooker.

Crock Pot Buffalo Chicken Lettuce Wraps

NUTRITIONAL INFORMATION

Serving Size: Size: 1/2 cup chicken + veggies

Calories: 147.7
Fat: 0.1 g
Carb: 5.2 g
Fiber: 1.6 g
Protein: 24.9 g
Sugar: 1.7 g
Sodium: 879 mg

Ingredients:
Ingredients For the chicken:

1 celery stalk

1 clove garlic

½ cup of hot cayenne pepper sauce (I prefer to use Frank's)

24 oz. of boneless skinless chicken breast

½ onion (diced)

16 oz. of fat free low sodium chicken broth

Ingredients For the wraps:

6 large lettuce leaves (preferably Bibb or Iceberg)

1 ½ cups of shredded carrots

2 large celery stalks (cut into 2 inch matchsticks)

Directions:

1. First, in a crock pot, **combine** chicken, onions, celery stalk, garlic and broth (note: enough to cover your chicken, use water if the can of broth isn't enough).
2. **After which you cover** and cook on high for 4 hours.
3. **After that, you remove** the chicken from pot, **reserve** ½ cup broth and discard the rest.
4. **Finally, you shred** the chicken with two forks, **return** to the slow cooker with the ½ cup broth and the hot sauce and **set** to on high for an additional 30 minutes.

It makes about 3 cups chicken.

Directions on how to prepare lettuce cups

1. **First, you place** ½ cup of buffalo chicken in each leaf, **top** with ¼ cup shredded carrots, celery and dressing of your choice.
2. After which you wrap up and start eating!

Slow Cooker Jalapeño Popper Chicken Chili
NUTRITIONAL INFORMATION

Serving Size: Size: 1 generous cup, 1 oz. avocado

Calories: 285
Fat: 12 g
Carb: 20 g
Fiber: 5 g
Protein: 25 g
Sugar: 1 g
Sodium: 350 mg

Ingredients:

3 cloves of minced garlic

2 jalapeños (with seeds removed)

1 lb. (about 93%) of lean ground chicken

2 teaspoons of smoked paprika

2 teaspoons of dried oregano

1 teaspoon of ground cumin

1 (about 14 oz.) of can petite diced tomatoes

Chopped scallions (for garnish)

4 oz. of goat cheese (it is optional)

1 medium white onion (diced)

1 red bell pepper (diced)

1 large sweet potato (about 14 oz.)

1 lb. (about 95%) lean ground beef

2 teaspoons of chili powder

2 teaspoons of kosher salt

¼ teaspoon of red pepper flakes

1 cup of reduced sodium chicken broth

8 oz. of diced avocado (from 2 small haas)

Directions:

1. First, you place all the ingredients except the scallion, avocado and goat cheese in the slow cooker and cook on low for 8 hours.
2. At this point when it is done, break up the ground meat with a wooden spoon and add half of the goat cheese if using.
3. Then you serve garnished with scallions and avocado on top.

Crock Pot Sesame Honey Chicken

NUTRITIONAL INFORMATION

Serving Size: Serving Size: over 2/3 cup
Calories: 185.5
Fat: 2 g
Protein: 27 g
Carbs: 13.5 g
Fiber: 0.7 g
Sugar: 10 g
Sodium: 504 mg

Ingredients:

Black pepper (to taste)

¼ cup of honey

3 tablespoons of rice wine vinegar

1 tablespoon of water

1 teaspoon of onion powder

1 heaping tablespoon of cornstarch

2 medium scallions (chopped for garnish)

2 lbs. of boneless, skinless chicken breast

1/3 cup of low-sodium soy sauce (preferably tamari for gluten-free)

¼ cup of tomato paste

2 cloves garlic (minced)

1 teaspoon of sesame oil

1 teaspoon of sriracha hot chili sauce (or better still more to taste)

¼ cup of water

½ tablespoon of sesame seeds

Directions:

1. First, you place the chicken in the slow cooker and season with black pepper.

2. After which in a medium bowl, you **combine** soy sauce, honey, vinegar, tomato paste, garlic, 1 tablespoon of water, sesame oil, onion powder and sriracha hot chili sauce.
3. **After that, you pour** over chicken and **cook** on LOW for 3-4 hours.
4. At this point, you **remove** chicken, leaving the sauce in the slow cooker.
5. **Then you shred** chicken with two forks; **set aside**.
6. Furthermore, in a small bowl, **dissolve** cornstarch in remaining ¼ cup water; **add** to the slow cooker and **stir** to combine.
7. **After which you cover** and **cook** on HIGH for about 15 to 20 minutes until slightly thickened; **return** chicken to the slow cooker and mix well.
8. Finally, you **serve** chicken and sauce over rice and **top** with sesame seeds and chopped scallions for garnish.

Enjoy!

Slow Cooker Lemon Feta Drumsticks

NUTRITIONAL INFORMATION

Serving Size: Size: 2 drumsticks
Calories: 195
Fat: 7 g
Carb: 3 g
Fiber: 0.5 g
Protein: 28 g
Sugar: 0.5 g
Sodium: 250 mg (without salt)

Ingredients:

kosher salt and fresh ground pepper

1 tablespoon of dried oregano

1/3 cup of feta cheese (fresh grated)

8 skinless chicken drumsticks (about 30 oz. total)

2 teaspoons of garlic powder

Juice of one lemon

Directions:

1. First, you season chicken with salt, garlic powder, pepper, oregano, and lemon juice.
2. After which you place in the slow cooker and cook on HIGH for 4 hours, or until chicken is no longer pink in the center near the bone.
3. At this point when chicken is cooked through, you sprinkle with grated feta.
4. Then you cover until cheese is melted.

   NOTE: *when I did mine, my drumsticks were small, I weighed the cooked meat off the bone on one and it weighed 2.5 oz.*

However, this is how I calculated points since there was no skinless on the bone option. If yours are larger you will need to adjust.

Embarrassingly Easy Crock Pot Salsa Chicken Thighs

NUTRITIONAL INFORMATION

Serving Size: Size: scant 1/2 cup
Calories: 187
Fat: 8 g
Carb: 3 g
Fiber: 1 g
Protein: 30 g
Sugar: 0 g
Sodium: 315 mg
Cholesterol: 127 mg

Ingredients:

1 cup of chunks salsa

¼ teaspoon of garlic powder

Salt (to taste)

1-1/2 lbs. of lean skinless chicken thigh filets (Perdue Fit and Easy)

Adobo seasoning (or better still salt) to taste

¾ teaspoon of ground cumin

Directions:

1. First, you season the chicken with adobo (or salt), then place in the crock pot and top with salsa, garlic powder and ½ teaspoon of cumin.
2. After which you cover and cook on LOW for about 4 hours.
3. At this point when it cooked, remove the chicken and set on a large plate; shred with two forks.
4. After that, you pour the liquid into a bowl and reserve, then place the shredded chicken back into the crock pot, adjust salt to taste and add remaining ¼ teaspoon of cumin.
5. Finally, you pour ¾ cup of the reserved liquid back into the crock pot and cover until ready to serve.
6. It makes about 2 ¾ cups of chicken.

Crock Pot Balsamic Pork Roast

NUTRITIONAL INFORMATION

Serving Size: Size: 3 oz. pork
Calories: 214
Fat: 12 g
Carb: 4 g
Fiber: 0 g
Protein: 21 g
Sugar: 3 g
Sodium: 196 mg
Cholet: 72 mg

Ingredients:
Kosher salt (to taste)

½ teaspoon of red pepper flakes

1/3 cup of balsamic vinegar

1 tablespoon of honey

2 pound of boneless pork shoulder roast (preferably sirloin roast)

½ teaspoon of garlic powder

1/3 cup of chicken (or better still vegetable broth)

1 tablespoon of Worcestershire sauce

Directions:

1. First, you season the pork with salt, garlic powder and red pepper flakes and place it into the slow cooker.
2. After which you mix together the broth and vinegar and pour it over the pork, then pour the honey over and set the timer for 4 hours on High or 6-8 hours on Low.
3. After that, once the pork is cooked and tender (NOTE: it should shred easily with a fork), remove from slow cooker with tongs into a serving dish.
4. Then you break apart lightly with two forks and put back into the slow cooker and ladle ½ cup sauce over the pork and keep warm until ready to eat.

Crock Pot Santa Fe Chicken
NUTRITIONAL INFORMATION

Serving Size: Size: 1 cup
Calories: 190
Fat: 1.5 g
Fiber: 5.6 g
Carbs: 23.1 g
Protein: 21 g

Ingredients:

About 14.4 oz. of can diced tomatoes with mild green chilies

8 oz. of frozen corn

About 14.4 oz. can of fat free chicken broth

1 teaspoon of garlic powder

1 teaspoon of cumin

Salt to taste

24 oz. (about 1 ½) lbs. of chicken breast

15 oz. of can black beans

¼ cup of fresh cilantro (chopped)

3 scallions (chopped)

1 teaspoon of onion powder

1 teaspoon of cayenne pepper (to taste)

Directions:

1. First, you **combine** chicken broth, beans (drained), corn, tomatoes, scallions, cilantro, garlic powder, onion powder, cumin, cayenne pepper and salt in the crock pot.
2. **After which you season** chicken breast with salt and lay on top.
3. After that you **cook** on low for about 10 hours or on high for 6 hours.
4. Then half an hour before serving, I suggest you **remove** chicken and **shred**.
5. **Furthermore, you return** chicken to slow cooker and stir in.
6. **After that, you adjust** salt and seasoning to taste.
7. **Finally, you serve** over rice or tortillas and your favorite toppings.

Easy Crock Pot Chicken and Black Bean Taco Salad

NUTRITIONAL INFORMATION

Serving Size: Size: 1 salad
Calories: 290
Fat: 9 g
Carb: 20 g
Fiber: 8 g
Protein: 34 g
Sugar: 1 g
Sodium: 521 mg
Cholesterol: 69 g

Ingredients:

1 tablespoon of reduced sodium taco seasoning

1 cup of chunks salsa

2 (about 16 oz. total) skinless, boneless chicken breasts

½ teaspoon of cumin

1 cup of canned black beans (rinsed)

Ingredient for the Salad:

½ cup of zesty avocado cilantro buttermilk dressing

6 cups of chopped romaine (or better still red leaf)

¼ cup of reduced Mexican cheese blend

Directions:

1. First, you place the chicken in the slow cooker and season with taco seasoning and cumin.
2. After which you pour the beans over the chicken and top with salsa.
3. After that, you cover and cook on LOW for about 4 hours, or until the chicken is tender and easily shreds with 2 forks.
4. At this point, you shred the chicken and combine with the beans and sauce, keep warm until ready to eat.

It makes about 3 ½ cups.

Directions on how to make the salad:

1. First, you place 1 ½ cups of lettuce on each plate.
2. After which you top with ¾ cup of chicken and bean mixture, 1 tablespoon of cheese and 2 tablespoons of zesty avocado buttermilk dressing.

Slow Cooker Taco Stew Meat

Ingredients

1 Onion (chopped)

1 can of Diced Tomatoes

2-3 Tablespoons of fresh chopped Cilantro

1 pound of Stew Meat

1-2 Cups of chopped Celery (NOTE: just a matter of taste how much)

1 package of Taco Seasoning

Directions:

1. First, you place all ingredients in slow cooker.
2. After which you cook on low for about 6 hours

Freezer Instructions

1. All you do is place all ingredients into freezer safe zip lock bag
2. Freeze
3. After which you thaw out for one night in refrigerator
4. Then you place partially thawed meal into slow cooker and cook on low for about 6 hours

Fish Tacos with Mango Salsa

Yield: 8-12 tacos depending on how much you fill them

Ingredients

1-2 Tablespoons of Creole seasoning

About 8-12 corn tortillas

½ recipe of mango salsa

Lime wedges for squeezing on the tacos

3-4 Tilapia fillets (it is about 1½ lbs. of fish)

1 Tablespoon of olive oil

2 cups of shredded cabbage

½ recipe of Cilantro Lime Crema

Directions:

1. First, you make the mango salsa and cilantro lime crema ahead of time and refrigerate until ready to use.
2. After which you add the 1 Tablespoon of olive oil to a skillet heat on medium.
3. After that, you cut the tilapia into bite-size chunks and coat in the creole seasoning.
4. Then you cook in the skillet for about 6-10 minutes, until done.
5. Finally, you serve immediately in tortillas with shredded cabbage, mango salsa, crema and a squeeze of lime.

Easy Shredded Pork over Caramelized Plantains

Ingredients For the crock pot pork:
1 yellow onion (sliced)

1 tablespoon of garlic powder

Salt and pepper (to taste)

2 lb. of pork loin

3 cups of beef broth

1 teaspoon of onion powder

Directions For the plantain mash:
2 tablespoons of coconut oil

Pinch of allspice

3-4 tablespoons of canned coconut milk

4 brown plantains (peeled, sliced in half lengthwise)

1 teaspoon of cinnamon

Pinch of salt

Directions:

1. First, you add all your pork ingredients to a crock pot and cook on low for 8-10 hours.
2. Then once your pork is done cooking, you use two forks and shred it to pieces.
3. At this point, you place a large skillet under medium heat and add coconut oil.
4. Furthermore, once the oil is melted and the skillet is hot, add your sliced plantains.
5. After which you sprinkle with cinnamon, allspice and salt.
6. Then you cook on both sides for about 4-5 minutes or until soft.
7. In addition, you add plantains to a food processor and puree, scraping down the sides if necessary.
8. After that, while the food processor is still running, pour in your coconut milk until you get a smooth plantain puree.
9. This is when you taste for seasoning.

10. Finally, if you want to serve, I suggest you add a scoop of plantain mash to plates and top with pork.
11. After which you garnish with sliced avocado and minced cilantro, if desired.

Crock Pot Kid-Friendly Turkey Chili

NUTRITIONAL INFORMATION

Serving Size: Size: 1 cup
Calories: 226
Fat: 3 g
Carb: 21 g
Fiber: 3.5 g
Protein: 31 g
Sugar: 5 g
Sodium: 688 mg

Ingredients:

1 teaspoon of oil

1 red bell pepper (diced fine)

1 ½ cups of frozen corn kernels

8 oz. of small can plain tomato sauce

1 teaspoon of cumin

½ teaspoon of kosher salt

1.3 lbs. (about 99%) lean ground turkey

1 medium onion (minced)

1 garlic clove (minced)

10 oz. of can Rotel Mild Tomatoes

¼ cup of low sodium chicken broth

½ teaspoon of chili powder

½ teaspoon of paprika

Optional Toppings:

Reduced fat sour cream

Baked tortilla chips

Diced avocado

Reduced fat shredded cheese

Directions:

1. First, you heat a large skillet over medium-high heat, add the turkey, season with salt and cook, breaking up with a spoon until turkey browns and is no longer pink.
2. After which you place into the slow cooker.
3. After that, you add the oil to the skillet and sauté the onion, garlic and bell pepper over medium heat for about 4 to 5 minutes.
4. Then you spoon over turkey into the slow cooker and stir in corn and tomatoes, tomato sauce, cumin, chili powder, paprika and salt, mix until well blended.
5. At this point, you pour the chicken broth into the crock pot and add the bay leaf.
6. This is when you cover and cook on HIGH 4 hours or LOW 6 hours.
7. Finally, you serve with desired toppings.

Honey Chili Chicken and Vegetables

Serves: 6 servings

Ingredients

1 teaspoon of kosher salt

2 tablespoons of canola oil

¼ Cup of soy sauce

¼ Cup of ketchup

1 tablespoon of lime juice

¼ Cup of cold water

2 ½ lbs. of boneless, skinless chicken breasts

¼ teaspoon of black pepper

1 Cup of honey

⅓ Cup of sweet chili sauce

2 teaspoons of garlic powder

8 Cup of frozen stir-fry vegetables

2 tablespoons of corn starch

Directions:

1. First, you season chicken with salt and pepper and brown in canola oil until lightly browned, but not cooked through.
2. After which you place chicken in slow-cooker.
3. After that, you combine honey, soy sauce, garlic powder, sweet chili sauce, ketchup, and lime juice and pour over chicken.
4. Then you cook on LOW for 3-4 hours or HIGH for 1½-2 hours.
5. At this point, you remove chicken from sauce, place on plate, and shred.
6. Furthermore, you add frozen vegetables to slow-cooker, cover and let cook on HIGH for about 20 minutes or until they are cooked through.
7. After that, you combine cornstarch and water and stir into sauce and vegetables.
8. This is when you return lid and cook for an additional 10 minutes or until sauce is thickened.

9. Finally, you return chicken to the sauce and vegetables and serve over steamed rice.

Easy Creamy Crock-Pot Chicken Tikka Masala

Ingredients

1 large onion (finely chopped)

2 tablespoons of grated fresh ginger

2 tablespoons of olive oil

2 teaspoons of ground cumin

2 teaspoons of paprika

½ teaspoon of cinnamon

½ teaspoon of ground black pepper

1 cup / 250 ml of heavy cream (or better still full-fat BPA-free coconut milk)

Juice of ½ a lemon

2 lbs. / 900 gr free-range organic chicken breasts (cut into 1½-inch chunks)

4 garlic cloves (minced)

1 (About 29 oz.) can of tomato sauce

1 tablespoon of Garam masala

2 teaspoons of ground coriander

1 teaspoon of turmeric

½ teaspoon of cayenne pepper (make sure you adjust according to your heat preference)

1 bay leaf

2 tablespoons of arrowroot powder

1. Remember that arrowroot powder acts like cornstarch (NOTE: you can use cornstarch if that's what you have in your pantry.)

Directions:

1. First, you grease the inside of your crockpot bowl with a bit of olive oil and set aside.
2. After which you combine all ingredients (except for bay leaves, heavy cream, arrowroot powder, and lemon juice) in a large bowl.
3. Then with a large spatula, stir to combine everything, making sure that the chicken is well coated.
4. After that, you pour the mixture into the slow cooker and place the two bay leaves on top.
5. At this point, you cover and cook for about 8 hours on low (or preferably 4 hours on high).
6. Furthermore, when done, in a small bowl combine heavy cream and arrowroot powder (or cornstarch), and gently stir into the mixture.
7. After that, you let cook an additional 20 minutes to thicken up.
8. Finally you add lemon juice and gently stir to incorporate.
9. Make sure you serve warm.

NOTE: you can store leftover in an airtight container in the fridge for up to 5 days.

NUTRITIONAL INFORMATION

Serving Size: (PER SERVING)

400 calories

18 grams of fat

6 grams of carbs

49 grams protein.

Lighter Buffalo Chicken Dip

NUTRITIONAL INFORMATION

Serving Size: **Serving Size:** 1/3 cup
Calories: 107.9
Fat: 4.9 g
Carbs: 5.4 g
Fiber: 0 g
Protein: 10.3 g

Ingredients:

1 cup of fat free sour cream

½ cup of crumbled blue cheese

4 oz. of reduced fat cream cheese (softened)

½ cup of Franks hot sauce (or better still whatever hot sauce you like)

1 teaspoon of white wine vinegar

2 cups (about 14 oz. Raw) of cooked shredded chicken

Directions:

1. First you m**ix** the first 5 ingredients together until smooth.
2. **After which you add** the chicken and put this in the crock pot on low for about 3-4 hours.
3. **After that, you serve** warm.
4. If you want to do this on the stove, I suggest you simmer on low heat 30 minutes.

CONCLUSION

Thanks for reading through this book; if you follow judiciously through the recipes outlined above, you will be working through the entire process of adopting a grain-free lifestyle, from purging your kitchens of grains, to shopping for wholesome foods, to making grain-free recipes.

Remember, the only bad action you can take is no action at all.

www.ingramcontent.com/pod-product-compliance
Lightning Source LLC
Chambersburg PA
CBHW081724100526
44591CB00016B/2496